Modern pictures and water-colour drawings

Manson & Woods Christie

Nabu Public Domain Reprints:

You are holding a reproduction of an original work published before 1923 that is in the public domain in the United States of America, and possibly other countries. You may freely copy and distribute this work as no entity (individual or corporate) has a copyright on the body of the work. This book may contain prior copyright references, and library stamps (as most of these works were scanned from library copies). These have been scanned and retained as part of the historical artifact.

This book may have occasional imperfections such as missing or blurred pages, poor pictures, errant marks, etc. that were either part of the original artifact, or were introduced by the scanning process. We believe this work is culturally important, and despite the imperfections, have elected to bring it back into print as part of our continuing commitment to the preservation of printed works worldwide. We appreciate your understanding of the imperfections in the preservation process, and hope you enjoy this valuable book.

MODERN PICTURES

AND

Water-colour Drawings,

THE PROPERTY OF A GENTLEMAN GIVING UP HIS TOWN RESIDENCE,

AND ALSO OF A LADY, DECEASED;

And IMPORTANT WORKS by the following Artists—

L. Alma Tadema, R.A.	T. S. Cooper, R.A.,	W. Mulready, R.A.,	G. Morland,
F. Madox Brown,	F. R. Lee, R.A.,	A. Fraser,	L. Perrault,
R. Burnier,	Sir F. Leighton, P.R.A.	J.W. Oakes, A.R.A.,	J. Portaels,
J. B. Burgess, R.A.,	Seymour Lucas, A.R.A.	J. F. Herring, Sen.,	C. Stanfield, R.A.
T. Creswick, R.A.,	E. Burne Jones,	W. Linnell,	A. Stannard,
A. Clint,	F. Lee Bridell,	F. Morgan,	W. C. Thomas,
	E. Verhoeckhoven:		

WHICH

Will be Sold by Auction by

MESSRS. CHRISTIE, MANSON & WOODS,

AT THEIR GREAT ROOMS,

8 KING STREET, ST. JAMES'S SQUARE,

On SATURDAY, JULY 8, 1893,

AT ONE O'CLOCK PRECISELY.

May be viewed Two Days preceding, and Catalogues had, at Messrs. CHRISTIE, MANSON and WOODS' Offices, 8, *King Street, St. James's Square, S.W.*

CONDITIONS OF SALE.

---o---

I. THE highest Bidder to be the Buyer; and if any dispute arise between two or more Bidders, the Lot so in dispute shall be immediately put up again and re-sold.

II. No person to advance less than 1s., above Five Pounds, 5s., and so on in proportion.

III. In the case of Lots upon which there is a reserve, the Auctioneer shall have the right to bid on behalf of the Seller.

IV. The Purchasers to give in their Names and Places of Abode, and to pay down 5s. in the Pound, or more, in part of payment, or the whole of the Purchase-Money, *if required*, in default of which, the Lot or Lots so purchased to be immediately put up again and re-sold.

V. The Lots to be taken away and paid for, whether genuine and authentic or not, with all faults and errors of description, at the Buyer's expense and risk, within Two days from the Sale, Messrs. CHRISTIE, MANSON and WOODS not being responsible for the correct description, genuineness, or authenticity of, or any fault or defect in, any Lot, and making no warranty whatever.

VI. To prevent inaccuracy in delivery, and inconvenience in the settlement of the Purchases, no Lot can on any account be removed during the time of Sale, and the remainder of the Purchase-Money must absolutely be paid on the delivery.

VII. Upon failure of complying with the above Conditions, the Money deposited in part of payment shall be forfeited, all Lots uncleared within the time aforesaid shall be re-sold by public or private Sale, and the deficiency (if any) attending such re-sale shall be made good by the Defaulter at this Sale.

CATALOGUE.

On SATURDAY, JULY 8, 1893,

AT ONE O'CLOCK PRECISELY.

WATER-COLOUR DRAWINGS.

D. COX

18/- 1 Old Cottages and Barn   8 x 10   *McLean*

F LEE BRIDELL

5/- 2 Southampton Water: Moonlight
       1 x 12

P DE WINT.

— — 3 A Gipsy Encampment   14 x 11   *Wigyell*

H. MOORE, R A., 1863.

'0 4 On the Ouse, Near York   12 x 18

H. MOORE, R A , 1865-80.

1/2 5 Sunset: Brading, Isle of White
       16 x 24

B 2

SIR J. REYNOLDS.

2£   6 Mrs. Crewe—*crayons*   20 × 20

J. M W. TURNER, R.A.

6 6   7 The Abbey Church, Bath, 1796
      9½ in. by 11 in
      Exhibited at the Royal Academy, 1796 (No. 715)
      Exhibited at Burlington House, 1887   Agnew

COPLEY FIELDING, 1847.

70   8 A Scotch Lake Scene, with figures and cows   Agnew
      11 × 14

D COX

9   8a Haddon Hall. Going out Hawking
      Exhibited at the Cox Exhibition, Birmingham, 1890
      From the Stone Ellis Collection
      5 × 12

D COX.

   8b The Terrace, Powis Castle
      From the Stone Ellis Collection
      11 × 12   } A Lea

D COX.

— —   8c Powis Castle
      From the Stone Ellis Collection
      14 × 10

BIRKET FOSTER

5 6   9 A Woody River Scene, with sheep and dog   Agnew
      9 × 17

E DUNCAN

8 6   10 Fishing Boats and Brig in a Squall   Kinnaird
      12 × 20

A. C. GOW, R A, 1871-2

190   11 THE FIRST PROVISION BOAT FOR THE BESIEGED   do
      TOWN   14 × 22

P DE WINT

40 12 BOLTON ABBEY AND RECTORY *Vokins*
    16¼ in. by 27 in
    Purchased from the Artist

SIR J. GILBERT, R A., 1866

85 13 AGINCOURT *McLean*

    King Henry   I tell thee truly, herald,
    I know not if the day be ours or no,
    For yet a many of your horsemen peer
    And gallop o'er the field
    Mountjoy.   The day is yours.
    King Henry   Praised be God, and not our strength for it !
    20 × 30   King Henry V, act iv scene 7

PICTURES.

J. BRETT, A.R.A

19 14 THE WHITESHELL POINT, Caswell Bay *Kennedy*
    6 × 10

J F. HERRING, SEN., 1861.

35 15 A STABLE-YARD, with a horse, goat, and poultry *Isaacs*
    20 × 24

G. B. O'NEILL

21 16 SPECTACLES FOR ALL SIGHTS AND AGES
    Exhibited at the Royal Academy, 1848
    24 × 18

H VAN RUITH.

24 17 THE BLESSING OF THE PALMS, Capri
    Exhibited at the Salon
    Exhibited at Leeds
    40 × 70

E HAYES, R.H.A.

9½ 18 SUNSET. Trevose Head, Cornwall *Buck & Rei*
    8 × 13

J BURR.

6 18A DONALD'S TONIC   11 × 8

VAL PRINSEP, A.R.A.

20   19 "Les Deux Amans il y en a toujours un qui Aime et l'autre qui se laisse Aimer"
70 x 50

J B BURGESS, R.A.

13   20 Zulina   *30 x 20*

W. DUFFIELD

1-   21 Fruit and Still Life *oval*
14 x 11

J BRETT, A.R.A

85   22 Sea Mists Drifting in Shore
Exhibited at the Royal Academy
30 x 60

Rowton (?)

F. R UNTERBERGER.

70   23 Torre del Grecco   *30 x 60*

Koekkoek

H. SCHLESINGER, 1855.

21   24 The Speaking Likeness   *30 x 20*

BARON H. LEYS, 1846.

10½   25 An Interior, with smoker   *6 x 8*

Polak Jr.

FRED MORGAN.

93   26 Don't be Frightened
Exhibited at the Royal Academy
60 x 40

Richardson

L. PERRAULT

12   27 The Widow   *45 x 36*

Lister

SEYMOUR LUCAS, A.R.A., 1873.

72   28 Fleeced   16 x 24

PROUT

  29 The Bridge of Sighs   20 x 14   *Russell*

H KOEKKOEK.

23   30 A Sea Piece, with shipping
         From the Shandon Collection
         12 x 16

FRED MORGAN.

35   31 Waiting   27 x 15   *Rowe*

L ALMA TADEMA, R A

40   32 The Mirror
         From the Collection of W. R Sandbach, Esq
         11 x 7

F. R LEE, R A

70   33 The Avenue at Althorp, Northampton
         40 in. by 56 in.
         Exhibited at the Royal Academy, 1852
         Exhibited at the Jubilee Exhibition at Manchester, 1887

J. WEBB, 1874-5.

80   34 BAMBOROUGH CASTLE   *Foster*
         60 x 90

W. LINNELL.

94   35 TRAMPING HARVESTERS   *Lister*
         43 in. by 63 in
         Exhibited at the Royal Academy, 1880

ROSA BONHEUR, 1887.

900   36 THE HOME IN THE PYRENEES
       25 in. by 39 in
       500 to start

J. CONSTABLE, R A

12   37 A RIVER SCENE, with boats and figures

9/2   38 A LANDSCAPE, with a cottage, and peasant on a road   *moody*
       Purchased from the family   10 × 11

6   39 A LANDSCAPE, with a windmill   4 × 10   *do*
       Purchased from the family

4/2   40 A RIVER SCENE with windmill

4/2   41 A RIVER SCENE Sunset—circle 8"

J. CONSTABLE, R.A.

50   42 THE JUMPING HORSE
       49 in by 39½ in

G. VINCENT, 1826.

280   43 A WOODY LANDSCAPE, with cattle crossing a brook
       18 × 20

P NASMYTH.

70   44 A WOODY LANDSCAPE, with cottage, and figures near a *Wigzell*
       rustic bridge   8 × 10

THE PROPERTY OF A LADY, *deceased.*

WATER-COLOUR DRAWINGS.

F MACKENZIE.

21 45 Interior of the Hall, Christ Church College, Oxford *Volum*
    16 x 18

W. MULREADY, R.A.

4½ 46 First Lover   6 x 5   *Kennedy*
    A sketch for the Picture

W. MULREADY, R.A.

5 47 A Church Door   12 x 9
   An early work

W. TURNER (of Oxford)

10 48 A Landscape   18 x 22   *Agnew*

PICTURES.

W MULREADY, 1829.

7 49 Puppies' Heads   6 x 8   *Gooden*

W. MULREADY, R.A.

2 50 Boys Firing a Toy Cannon
   A sketch   7 x 9

W. MULREADY, R.A., 1826

310 51 THE ORIGIN OF A PAINTER

31 in by 26½ in.

Purchased from the painter, and has never been out of the family of the first owner

100 to start

W. MULREADY, R.A.

150 52 THE CARPENTER'S SHOP

Purchased from the painter, and has never been out of the family of the first owner

Exhibited at the British Institute, 1809

Exhibited at the International Exhibition, 1862

100 to start 36 × 26

C. STANFIELD, R.A.

250 53 ISOLA BELLA, Lago Maggiore   *Vokins*

28 in. by 44 in.

Exhibited at the Royal Academy, 1842

T. STOTHARD, R.A.

38 54 THE DANCE: a scene from Boccaccio   *do*

40 in by 51 in.

Purchased from the painter's studio, and has never been exhibited

THE PROPERTY OF A GENTLEMAN.

T FAED, R A.

28   55 Rest on the Way   8×7   *Wallis*

J F. HERRING, Sen., 1851.

6   56 A Hen and Chickens   10×8   *Lister*

E. VERBOECKHOVEN, 1859.

7 6   57 A Landscape, with sheep and lambs   20×26   *Polak Jr*

J. B BURGESS, R A.

3 6   58 The Present and the Future Returning from church   36×28

R. BURNIER.

10   59 A Grand Heath Scene in Holland, with cattle and sheep on a road   60×80

A. CLINT.

7   60 Sunset off Hastings   20×28

T. CRESWICK, R A.

11   61 The Approach to Llyn Idwal   8×9

T. CRESWICK, R.A.

25   62 Road at Ballachulish   6×8   *Moody*

T CRESWICK, R.A.

10/½   63 GROUSE SHOOTING, on the moors, near Whitby   *Hebdin*

T. S. COOPER, R.A., 1853.

128   64 A LANDSCAPE, with cows   *Vokins*
            30 x 36

T S COOPER, R A, 1856

5-6   65 A LANDSCAPE, with cows Twilight
            30 x 36

T. S. COOPER, R.A., 1856.

132   66 CANTERBURY MEADOWS, with cow, goat and sheep   *Agnew*
            20 x 24

T. S. COOPER, R.A.

8½   67 A LANDSCAPE, with bull, cows and sheep   *Richards*

The first picture painted by him after his return to England—obtained from the artist's brother
            11 x 14

13

*The following are
the Property of A GENTLEMAN, giving up
his residence in London.*

PICTURES

A. EGG, R.A.

11   68 THE DUCHESS OF MARLBOROUGH—circle 9"   *McLean*

W. P. FRITH, R.A.

69 HEAD OF A GIRL   6 × 5   *Hill*

C. BAXTER.

13   70 THE BRACELET   18 × 12   *Lister*

F. LEE BRIDELL, 1861.

8   71 VIEW ON ~~THE COAST OF THE MEDITERRANEAN, with Turkish boats and figures~~ Lake Como
19 in. by 23 in.

J. W. OAKES, A.R.A.

28   72 HASTINGS BEACH, with fishing boats   *Vicars*
13½ in. by 23½ in.

T. CRESWICK, R.A.

31   73 TINTAGEL, Cornwall
17 in. by 23 in.

J. BARRETT.

7   74 "CON AMORE"
27½ in. by 35½ in.
Exhibited at the Royal Academy, 1854

W. CAVE THOMAS.

29

75 Domenico da Peschia urges Savonarolo to resort to Ordeal by Fire for a Miraculous Confirmation

    38 *in.* by 32 *in*

J ARCHER, R S A.

41

76 Mort d'Arthur

    33 *in* by 38 *in*

    Exhibited at the International Exhibition, 1862

J ARCHER, R.S.A , 1859

25

77 Lady Jane Beaufort

    40 *in.* by 22 *in*

J ARCHER, R S A

31

78 THE SANCGREALL

    "King Arthur healed of his greavous wound in the island valey of Avalon"

    "It is a holy vessel that is born by a maiden, therein is a part of the holy blood of our Lord Jesus Christ, blessed might he bee, but it may not be seene, said Sir Ector, but if he bee by a perfect man."
                        History of King Arthur, vol iii c 14

    39½ *in.* by 62 *in.*

    Exhibited at the Royal Academy, 1863

FORD MADOX BROWN.

58

79 CHRIST WASHING PETER'S FEET

    47 *in.* by 53 *in*

    Prize awarded at Liverpool

    Exhibited at the Art Treasures Exhibition, Manchester, 1857

    From the Plint Collection, 1862

H. DAWSON, Sen., 1860.

80 80 ST. PAUL'S, from Southwark Bridge
54 in. by 85 in.

J. W. OAKES, A R A

81 MARCHLLYN-MAWR
"A solitary pool fringed round with rushes wild
43 in by 60 in.
Exhibited at the International Exhibition, 1862

J W OAKES, A R A

82 THE WARREN
The cony from the sand bank
Has run a rapid race
Through thistle, bent and tangled fern,
To seek the open space

35 in by 50 in
From the Plint Collection, 1862

SIR F LEIGHTON, P R A.

83 JEZEBEL AND AHAB, having caused Naboth to be put to death, go down to take possession of his vineyard, they are met at the entrance by Elijah the Tishbite

"Hast thou killed, and also taken possession"

94 in. by 91 in
Exhibited at the Royal Academy 1863

JOCARON.

84 The Dutch Fleet in a Fresh Breeze, with a view of Rotterdam in the distance
35 in by 60 in.
Bought by Peter the Great at Amsterdam, and presented by the Empress Catherine to Count Orloff
From the Collection of the Hon M. C. Maxwell

The following are the Property of A GENTLEMAN

PICTURES.

E BRISTOW.

2 1   85 Sportsman at an Inn Door   *9 × 11*   *McLean*

A EGG, R A.

86 The Farm Yard—*a sketch*   *5 × 9*

4

T. LUNY, 1836

87 A Coast Scene, with men-of-war at anchor, and The Companion   *11 × 12 each*   2

T. LUNY.

2 ½   88 The Vixen Gun Brig, passing Sombro Lighthouse, Nova Scotia   *10 × 12*

E. J. NIEMANN.

9   89 Richmond Castle, Yorkshire   *10 × 14*   *Helmsley*

J PORTAELS

5 ½   90 Maries de Bourg de Batz, Bretagne   *70 × 50*

A. STANNARD.

10   91 A Landscape, with peasants at a gravel pit, and cows in the distance   *22 × 30*   *Russell Norwich*

P. NASMYTH, 1818.

6 4   92 View of the Miller's Lynn at Inverary   *22 × 30*   *McLean*

17

VAN HUYSUM.

35   93 A Vase of Flowers, on a marble slab   24×18   *Russell*

HONDICOETER.

29   94 Borrowed Plumes   50×60   *do*

ANOTHER PROPERTY.

PICTURES.

3   95 Interior, with monkey and figures   16×12   *Hebden*

G. DURA.

2 4   96 A Pair of Views near Naples—*body colours*, &c.   10×12   4

BACKHUYSEN.

5   97 A Landscape, with peasant and animals   18×12   *Lister*

E. C. BARNES.

14   98 The Pet Bird   36×24   *do*

E C. BARNES.

7   99 Making a Bouquet   24×30   *Hebden*

R. CRAEYVANGER.

5½   100 The Return   36×50

C. CUNÆUS.

6½   101 A Dog and Poultry   18×24

C. DOLCE (After).

5 —   102 Mater Dolorosa   24×18   *Hill*

c

A. FRASER, R S A , 1828.

2 2 103 The Fisherman's House 24 × 36   M'Lean

GAINSBOROUGH

1 — — 104 Portrait of a Naval Officer 14 × 9

S P. JACKSON

5/2 105 A Coast Scene, with shipping (Watercolour) 12 × 20   Hill

F. DE LEUB

3/2 106 Children with a Dog 10 × 7   Hebdue

H. LIVERSEEGE.

? × 12 6 107 The Blessing 14 × 11   Misel

OTTO

4/2 108 A Winter Scene in Bavaria 26 × 32

A. F. PAYNE.

3/2 109 Ages Ago 50 × 36

S. PERCY

2 110 A Winter Scene 12 × 20

H REDMORE

6/2 111 A Sea Piece 22 × 34   Lister

H REDMORE.

7 112 A Calm, with shipping 22 × 34   do

J SYMONS
113 North Head, Auckland Harbour 16×24 — Murel

J. WAINWRIGHT
114 A Fruit Piece 20×14 — do

J. WARD, R.A.
115 Hastings Beach squally day 9×10 — A Smith

T. WHITTLE
116 Near Bettws-y-Coed 14×18 — Hebden

T WHITTLE.
117 The Sand Bank 14×18 — do

T. WHITTLE.
118 Summer Showers on the Medway 15×18 — do

E. C. WILLIAMS.
119 Old Mill on the Yare 9×10 — Lister

FINIS.

London: Printed by William Clowes & Sons, Limited, Stamford Street and Charing Cross